BECOMING LYLA DORE

BECOMING
Lyla Dore

poems

TERI YOUMANS GRIMM

RED HEN PRESS | PASADENA, CA

Book layout by Marcia Langren & Latina Vidolova

Library of Congress Cataloging-in-Publication Data

Names: Grimm, Teri Youmans, author.
Title: Becoming Lyla Dore / Teri Youmans Grimm.
Description: First edition. | Pasadena, CA : Red Hen Press, [2016]
Identifiers: LCCN 2015046623 | ISBN 9781597093224 (softcover : acid-free paper)
Subjects: | BISAC: POETRY / General.
Classification: LCC PS3607.R564 A6 2016 | DDC 811/.6—dc23
LC record available at http://lccn.loc.gov/2015046623

The National Endowment for the Arts, the Los Angeles County Arts Commission, the Los Angeles Department of Cultural Affairs, the Dwight Stuart Youth Fund, the Pasadena Arts & Culture Commission and the City of Pasadena Cultural Affairs Division, the Ahmanson Foundation, and Sony Pictures Entertainment partially support Red Hen Press.

First Edition
Published by Red Hen Press
www.redhen.org

Acknowledgments

Grateful acknowledgment is made to the editors of the publications in which these poems first appeared, some in earlier forms:

Bridge Eight: "At Kalem's Headquarters, the Roseland Hotel," "On the Train to Hollywoodland," and "Star Dust"; *burntdistrict*: "I Wasn't Pregnant, Dr. Moore Explained . . ." and "This Is How It Ends"; *Green Mountains Review*: "The Devil's Passkey" and "A Visit from the Snake Man"; *Perversion*: "Angel's Tit," "On Being Given a Monkey Fur Coat from a Suit-or," "The Last Veil," and "When Theda Bara Came to Town"; *South Dakota Review*: "Go on, Please. This Is Very Interesting," "Lyla Recalls That Summer," and "Magic Lantern"; *Sugar House Review*: "My Mother Tells Me I Was Conceived in Fire before I Was Condemned by It," "*Photoplay* Brains and Beauty Contest Photograph," and "Refrain."

The following recorded poems appeared online at the website www.eatwords.net:

"At the Station," "The Devil's Passkey," "I Wasn't Pregnant, Dr. Moore Explained . . . ," "Lyla Recalls That Summer," "My Mother Tells Me I Was Conceived in Fire before I Was Condemned by It," "*Photoplay* Brains and Beauty Contest Photograph," "Refrain," "This Is How It Ends," and "When Kalem Studios Came to Town."

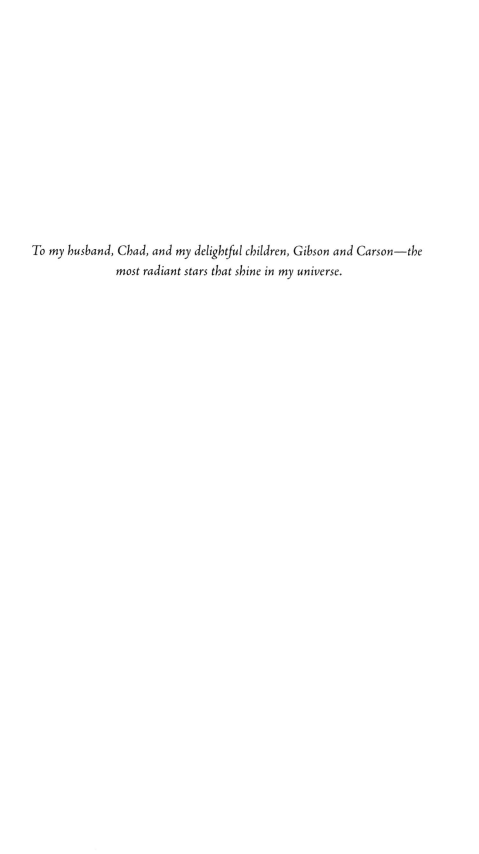

To my husband, Chad, and my delightful children, Gibson and Carson—the most radiant stars that shine in my universe.

CONTENTS

Becoming Lyla Dore

Magic Lantern

Forget what you know about faded stars,
about curiosities and relics.
This is about magic.
Back when there was such a thing,
my father made a living
as a lanternist. I'd go with him
to the Imperial where between comedy reels
he'd show glass slides of the Taj Mahal
or lovers kissing in a Venetian gondola. Familiar
scenes too and after the flickering black and grey,
unexpected colors glazed the screen and one
could watch a frozen landscape deliquesce into spring,
lilacs move by a perceptible wind, a rabbit disappear
into a hole and the lake reacquainting everyone with blue.
There was a time before I was born,
my father was the whole damn show,
when the magic lantern made the common seem new.
But he was eclipsed by the Kinetoscope,
the Cinematograph, by a world
that seemed to spin only toward new
pleasures. Relegated to sing-a-longs
and advertisements, when my father flashed slides
for trusses, the local dentist, lyrics
to "Shine on Harvest Moon," well, there was no magic
left then, was there? I was embarrassed
that what he had to offer was no longer desired.
I was at an age to understand desire.
Sitting in a darkened theater with strangers
watching people live on screen, larger than ourselves,
real but not real, and at the same time

to feel someone's hand brush my own, accidentally or no—
their shoulder pressed into mine as they shifted in their seat,
breath warm on my neck gave me more than a taste
for intimacy. To be watched like that, to touch and be
touched all at once until the body and the image
of the body fused. In that cavernous stupor
even the way I dreamed was changed forever.
Like the magician's assistant that disappears
into a cabinet then reappears in another
part of the theater, I left my seat in the dark,
mingled with the dust in the funnel of light and
created myself in my own image on the screen.
Before arc light and electric bulbs, the lantern's glow
came from an oxygen and hydrogen flame fixed
on a cylinder of lime. Combustible, surely, but the illusion
blazed brighter! To be in limelight is to become incandescent
in the alchemy of dangerous gas and mineral, to smolder
in another's mind or heart. I would have risked setting
myself on fire, if it meant the world could see me better.

But that was before I knew better.

WHEN KALEM STUDIOS CAME TO TOWN

Movies filled with the thrills of living
placed a camera on the banks of Strawberry Creek,
placed Union and Rebel soldiers there,
placed barefoot Crackers and smelted stills,
Seminoles and pistol-toting lawmen,
alligators and bobcats, egrets and egret
hunters. Into a box they captured
the light of Jacksonville sun and turned
gesture into spectacle, the marvel of bodies
in motion. Into a box they captured
the light of Jacksonville sun and consecrated
with golden halos the daughters of orange
growers, misers, deacons and drunkards.
These actresses leaned so prettily against
the bridge's rails and fought off scoundrel's
kisses. On the banks of Strawberry Creek
were so many smudge pots
it looked like the swamp was all ablaze.
The Movies brought so much mayhem
to our bluff, but few of us complained!
Least of all me. The man who controlled
the camera once stood me on a crate, held
my hand in his and helped me crank, humming
a tune so the action wouldn't lose its rhythm.
I peered into the glass and saw for the first time,
a world within the world, finer and more distinct.
Horses leapt twenty feet from the bridge
draped with smoke and so many Union
dead it felt as though we may win, after all,
a war long fought and decided.
It was a wonder! The box so powerful
it could change our own history.

Phantasmagoria

I never feared the shadows cavorting
in my room—nanny-goats and vultures,
jellyfish and centaurs—nor the hands
that made them. They hardly seemed
related, father's contorted fingers, a witch
riding a broom, a bear on a swing.
What appeared on my walls was as real
as if those things were right behind me.

My father created magic
for our pleasure with spinning
chandeliers of twigs, harnessed
light and wind that turned
a drawing of a horse into a stampede
of ghosts galloping along my bed.
A tin can full of tiny
holes and light exploded
into a universe that breathed
stars so thick, they could have filled
three skies, their pulsing formed
a tornado from crêpe paper
twisting over a parade of small circus
animals staunchly fixed in place,
but their shadow selves were frenzied,
aware of the dooming sky.

Emanating from a piece of etched tin,
a sideways figure-eight of light
swirled on the back of my door.
Look at that snake! I said.
But father told me there were many

snakes devouring each other.
I turned my head and squinted.
They signify forever, he said.
I tried to see it his way,
but could only distinguish
the one, its many selves
slipping from its skin over and
over and over and over and over.

A Visit from the Snake Man

Outside my bedroom window, beneath the sound
of wind and dry leaves, a shadow called
my name—*Willie, Willie.* No relation to any tree
or shrub in the yard, he was a wanderer, friend
of the moon. He entered my room and said my name
once more, slow and on one note so it sounded
like the foghorns of ships that pass in the river,
familiar. "How do you do?" I asked and asked
once more when he didn't respond. *Your name
doesn't suit you. One day you'll be called something else.*
He moved about like a nosy guest, pausing at my dresser,
peering inside my armoire, lingering by the window.
"Sometimes you look like a man carrying a satchel
and then like a snake slithering up my wall." *And the moon
lights you up like a ghost. I can nearly see right through you.*
I looked down at my nightgown, my bare arms. I was
glowing like a corpse candle, translucent blue.
"I'm luminous," I said and knew it. His shadow covered
me like a blanket as if to put me out. *Just like the moon, Willie,
you have a dark side too* and he stayed there above me, shifting
from man to snake and back again before disappearing in a cloud.
But I knew he would return. Sure as shine.

Gathering of Ghosts

It was a Halloween tradition for father to make the underworld
appear. With Henry's help and some magic lanterns,
a skeleton rose from a cauldron, pointing its shaky finger
at the crowd. A woman shrouded in white glistered
on a screen of smoke, her red heart beating faster and
faster until she turned to fire. In front of a box a man
knelt, sprung the latch and demons leapt out at him
with sharpened tongues and jagged teeth.

I played the ghost fiddle behind a curtain.
The sound made my teeth hurt.

Across the rows of chairs, a four-foot spider crawled, I saw
Mrs. Moore attempt to swat it away from the twins.

There was a time it was forbidden in some towns, that sound
too distressing on the nerves.

> *If you steal with a pumpkin light*
> *Into a closet unseen*
> *In the mirror will appear the face*
> *Of your true lover on Halloween.*

When she emerged, Dulcie said she saw Bobby Harron
or maybe it was plain old Ernest Bradshaw with nicer hair.

Harmless as it all may seem, it's never a good idea
to conjure demons, even fake ones.
Mrs. Moore said to a flock of hens.

Dulcie said her mother wouldn't allow her
to wear a costume. But she did
let her have a mask. It was on a lorgnette
and covered her face in silver and white.
I thought it was elegant.

I was dressed like the Mountain Girl from *Intolerance*.
Though everyone surmised I was a wood nymph.
(*She must be freezing walking around with bare arms like that.*)
Mostly there were witches and cats.

A demon riding a demon swooped and soared over heads.

Opening the door even a little, invites the tempter into your home.

Put on a cape, my mother said repeatedly. Which I did and took it off again.

Henry made all of the scary demons appear and disappear, I said loudly.
He sees the world differently than others do, my father said.

Dr. Moore told me I was every bit as charming as the Mountain Girl.

> *On Halloween look in the glass*
> *Your future husband's face will pass.*

Father said Phantasmagoria means a gathering of ghosts.
In the mirror I saw a skeleton, but told no one.
It's apt, I remember thinking. We'll all be dead one day.

During Mrs. Hallard's recitation of "Ulalume,"
I knocked over a stack of plates accidentally.
Can't you go an hour without being the center of attention? Mother yelled.

Dr. Moore helped me pick up the dishes. His eyes reminded me
of Mr. Olcott, the director at Kalem.
Mother found my cape again.
It was strange I hadn't noticed the resemblance before.

Must you make a spectacle of yourself?
(I think it was really her who made one of me.)

Mother was pregnant five times before I came along.
None of them lived to see the world.
It was as though she found me perverse
to have made a home where none could thrive before.

Father said she spent all her love on the babies
who were never born. By my reckoning
it should have made her love me more.

It's not your fault, Willie, Dr. Moore whispered,
you were born to be a spectacle.

Dulcie and I walked home that evening.
She was worried about her mother's words.
What if we really were followed home by demons?

Then we should dance for them, I said, twirling her around.

We said goodbye in her front yard. I turned around to wave
and she was dipping and spinning,
her mask a shimmer in the moonlight.

Will-o'-the-wisp! Will-o'-the-wisp!
I pointed and yelled.

She threw the mask down shrieking and ran inside.
But I couldn't leave it on the wet ground,
the mask so elegant.
I hung it up on their front door.

Later on, I suspect, she thought me evil for it.

At Kalem's Headquarters, the Roseland Hotel

Silence held sway over the room
when Mr. Olcott ran that bit of film.

I'd nearly forgotten that afternoon,
the day's work completed, everyone stilled

by the swath of May's suppressing heat.
Sun filled spaces between branches

and leaves of the sweet-gum I sat beneath,
eating strawberries from a tin. Henry, knowing

there was unused film left in the camera,
turned it on me, quietly, well not on me

exactly, but on the light and the way
it presented itself upon me.

I wanted to give him something else,
something more than a girl eating beneath

a tree, so I looked into the camera and thought
real thoughts. Henry raised his hand to shade

the glare from the white sandy path nearby
and I saw him smile at the effect it had.

No one paid any attention to us, him
learning how to manipulate light

and shadow into feeling. Me, learning
how to take feeling and speak it through

a gaze. Later, on that torn canvas screen,
in a room full of people who understood

or thought they understood the power
of an image moving, was a moment,

recognized by all of us, of what it means
to remember and be remembered.

THE FILMING OF *The Clarion*

At the front doors of the saloon,
it was clear the pretend mob
had become a real one. The crowd
of mostly men and boys smashed
through windows, poured in,
broke the necks off liquor bottles
and drank with gusto, throwing
the heavy glass corks into the horde,
with no care as to where they landed.

Thus began the throwing of chairs and
mugs, while all around glass was breaking—
mirrors and bottles. The forty policemen
on hand were equipped only with rubber batons,
getting paid extra not to hurt anyone, while all
around the crowd seemed intent on tearing
the place down, with little to incite them,

She must have caught me from the
corner of her eye. Hanging laundry
in the backyard, perhaps when I
rounded the bend. Wearing her dress,
her hat, she would have known
where I was going. My disobedience
flagrant because even my father had
told me no.

Her ire, so far up, leaving
the wet clothes in the basket,
storming to her room to be sure

I took her things. Seething, it grew
clear how to punish me and
I'm certain it calmed her,
flaunting her authority so neatly.

save the director yelling *Action,*
and how quickly they responded
to their charge to *BE DESTRUCTIVE!*
Henry and I tried to get out of the way,
but he was knocked down
by an upended table. A woman shoved
me as she made toward the bar. I elbowed
her off and she ripped the sleeve
of my mother's dress, scratching my arm
in the process. Henry and I crouched,
headed to the front door and huddled there
with the onlookers who'd gathered
to watch the melee unfold.

She tore the pennants off my wall—
Viola Dana, Frances X. Bushman,
Charlie Chaplin, Marie Doro,
Blanche Sweet, Dustin Farnum—
all of them—cut up into
unrecognizable features with her
shears. From my armoire and under
my bed, she gathered all my
magazines and put them in a
washtub filled with water.

Henry and I looked at each other
stunned. This film company,
not one we knew well.
He'd wanted to see how a large
crowd scene was filmed, and I'd
come because it felt like
an adventure, pretending
to be older, seeing if I could pass.

In went my cosmetics, my entire
collection of lobby cards and
Movy-dols. Was it an act of mercy
or meanness that compelled her
to leave my Kalem scrapbook alone?
Either way, it was made clear to
everyone that I wasn't to work
around the lot anymore.

When the cameras positioned around the bar
ran out of film and the director yelled *Cut!*
Then *STOP! STOP!* It was like watching people
wake from an enchantment, coming back
to their senses, in awe at the destruction
around them, wondering how it all had happened.
They shook their heads and felt their bruises,
looked for hats that had been lost
in the commotion. The glass crunching
beneath their feet, sheepish folks waited
in line for their payment, while others,
still buzzing over what had occured,

needed to recount it over and over.
The cut on Henry's brow, he would
get away with. My mother's torn dress?
My scratched-up arm? Just as sure as
the dollar in my hand, I knew
that I would pay.

But I didn't need her consent
for this: to make the world my set,
to let daily life become the backdrop
through which I moved, until
everything became posture and
response, every movement intended
as if for the screen, a self-
awareness so practiced, it became
natural, each expression a captivating
close-up. I spoke, but softly.
Even my mother, who grew to hate
the sight of me, would agree—
you could not look away.

WHEN THEDA BARA CAME TO TOWN

An Indian prince once gave her a bracelet,
serpent shaped, with a secret compartment
that held poison. To a young suitor
she showed the hidden spring and he took it
from her hands, held it to his lips,
then died at Theda's feet.
I nearly swallowed my chewing gum
when I first read that story in a magazine.
And to think here she was! The actress born
in the shadow of the sphinx, the vampire
appearing in front of the Rialto where just days
before I'd thrilled at her horridness
in *The Tiger Woman*—a Russian princess
ruins her husband, connives a lover
into killing his own father, connives another
into killing himself before she comes
to her own bad end. I had to brace myself
against the grandstand so as not to be
crushed by the enraptured thousands.
Vamp for us, Theda! C'mon, let your hair down!
A man near me yelled and it was then
I realized the woman in the Sunday dress
and hat shaped like an oversized paper boat was her!
Reconciling the two women challenged me.
Others seemed to feel the same because
their faces, like mine, were puzzled
as she went on smiling kindly, blowing
sweet kisses. Still, everyone cheered, thrilled
to be in the presence of someone evil beloved.
But wasn't it just a hoax? I didn't care
if her mother really was a French actress,
her father an Italian sculptor or if her childhood

was spent among the pyramids of Egypt.
It didn't matter if the anagram of her name
meant *Arab Death*, if her rooms were swathed
in tiger skins and veils, or if she always slept
with a statue of Amen-Ra—
before this, it felt like it *could* be true.
It was gripping to watch her create
such glorious far-fetched destruction—
decency leagues protesting nearly every one
of her films, insisting they must not end
with Theda triumphant. But even those women
denouncing her, didn't they perhaps go home
and roll their shoulders, let their slips slip down,
dropping their gaze in the mirror? Didn't husbands
tell their wives that no man would fall for such
claptrap, but didn't they too, in private, wonder
what it would be like to have that body
draped on theirs, overpowered
by all that hair and flesh desiring? It was,
I decided, a different kind of deceit
that could make me love her more.
We begged her to show us through
filmy clothes and hungry mouth
what it is to live unfettered. But there
she was, demure, and pleasant face delighting
in our admiration. Living two lives as one!
I waved furiously, smiling, willing her gaze
to meet mine, until she nodded my way,
and I imagined her bestowing that gift to me.
A life with emerald eyes, diamond scales,
a secret chamber, golden and perilous.

I Recall That Summer

This begins the story that only plays inside my head.
To tell it makes me anxious. Words disintegrate
in air, then what? This memory turns to dust,
floats away on my breath? If only.

I'll give you the scenario straight
and where you'll see patterns neatly determined
as a tile floor, I'll see a mosaic of colored glass
that cuts and stones fit for a penitent's shoes.
Private hurts satisfy and it did please me
to take care of my neighbor's family. Mrs. Moore
had a sick mother in Perry. I'd just turned sixteen
so I could do the laundry and cook the meals,
send the children out to play, make uncomfortable
small talk with Dr. Moore about his day before I went home.

I liked washing dishes by that window.
The patch of dandelions at the edge of the woods
looked like a green sky full of small suns.
I liked sitting on the porch sewing a button,
snapping peas. But as weeks passed, I grew bored
and thus bolder, with Dulcie and the twins gone for hours,
and Henry, who knows where? As though it embarrassed
them to see me play the handmaiden.

I'd sit at her vanity, a smear of lipstick, try on her
jewelry and her dresses. I ironed his shirts
and placed a jar of flowers on his dresser,
dripped lavender water onto his pillow, left a strand
of my hair. You see the pattern, don't you? That thing
I do, that gesture to get someone's attention?

It was inevitable he'd show up one afternoon, find me
wearing silk from her bottom drawer. He locked the door
and leaned against the wall, hands behind him.
I'll only go so far with this. He told me to do things
to myself and without hesitation, I did them and I could
see myself in the mirror as I did them and I could see him
against the wall watching me and I could see me watching
him watching me watching him watching me—
I was dizzy, an over-wound toy, until I curled my finger at him
and he and he and he and I came loose. Fixed and broken
at the same time. I felt clean inside.

Later, I burned the sheet in a barrel out back. It went up
in an instant, as if it were made to start fires
and I wondered how long it would take for me
to be consumed like that. A question for the devil,
I guessed. Through the smoke I saw smaller puffs
of smoke as though a small train were headed
west through the field. But it was only the dandelions.
In a matter of hours they had turned. I picked a handful,
made complicated wishes and blew. As they fell apart
in the breeze I told the wind to carry them that way.
And I knew summer would go on that way. The bare
stems I put in a jar on his dresser.

Days later when I cut my hand open slicing onions,
I decided housework and children were a distraction.
His desire and my reflection became the only things
that mattered. What was real and what was illusion
collided in the mirror, like an accident,
but a compelling one—before it's determined
who's responsible, before the victims are named.

I Wasn't Pregnant, Dr. Moore Explained, Merely Late and This Procedure, While Painful, Would Resolve the Matter *or* Becoming Lyla Dore

My body was there, lying
hidden beneath the porch,
curled up like a wounded dog, blood
seeping through gauze, my underthings,
my ruined striped skirt,
making small rivulets in the sand.

A lie was there too, a hovering
shadow, shaped like a present. It floated
in midair like a hummingbird
and inside I heard scratching
and wings flapping as though
something was trying to get out.

Nothing was left inside of me.
But I was no longer a me,
no longer a girl, no longer good,
because nothing good
would make a mess like this.

A young woman was there,
beautiful as any star, standing in the
yard in front of a white door
that could have led anywhere.
She flickered in wind and moonlight.
I recognized her—my cheekbones. my lips,

my eyes—but not mine too. A gaze like that!
Shameless and kind. Able to cause
a saint to sin or even a saint's mother.

A lie emptied, a lie can fill.
The breath of her voice was a force in my body,
the way his body was once a force in mine,
the way his body spoke to me in moans and sighs.

Lie. Love. Leave. Lie. Love. Leave.
There was no place left for me but her.

Refrain

We stood about in our nightclothes, ghosts at a bonfire,
house disappearing and reappearing in the flames,
like a demon's magic trick, the firemen, unwitting assistants.
The rest of us stared wide-eyed at the destruction, useless
and worse, some saying what shouldn't have been said at all.
It hardly seemed time for an accounting of who had perished
and who had lived. *Dr. Moore is in Atlanta, I heard . . . Praise God,*

Dulcie seems unhurt . . . the twins, I hope, were first overcome by smoke,
sweet angels . . . Henry lost an eye trying to save them . . . was blown clear
from the second floor window . . . poor, dear Mrs. Moore, undone for weeks
over talk that's going around. There was nowhere for me to hide
and to have thrown myself into the fire would not have satisfied
anyone, but only cheated them of something more abiding.
Mrs. Dunn, her face turning mulish in the haze, said, *Well,*

I wouldn't be surprised in the least if Mrs. Moore did it to punish him.
A shadow added behind her, *That one there, she may not have lit the match,*
but she sure provided the fuel. And in a breath, those words became the truth,
spread from one cluster of folks to another. Father nudged me towards
mother who'd already begun the walk home. Is it true? Did I do all of this?
Dear Henry, the right side of his face burned, empty. Dulcie, arms
outstretched, untouchable as an angel in her impossibly white

nightgown, wailing for her dead. *I'm sorry,* I said, but it was lost in her
sorrow, the fire's roar, the ground beneath me shaking with the Devil's
laughter. The neighbors who cooed over me as a baby, fretted
my measles and scarlet fever, now turned their backs as I faltered
past them towards home. But I knew them well. And too soon
they'd leave behind this gutting loss, the Moores recalled with only
a tsk-tsk, and a shake of heads. But they remembered me,

incendiary girl, desire's wayward spark and made of me an example
for their sons and daughters. Tragedy faded as palmettos stemmed
through the ashes and pine seedlings began their journey upwards
and dogwoods took shelter beneath the oaks and warblers filled
the trees with song, but they were left with their own song,
one they handed down like china: *Though she didn't light the match,
Willie was the fuel.* That clever refrain outliving us all.

Photoplay BRAINS AND BEAUTY
CONTEST PHOTOGRAPH

I painted my lips a vigorous red and discomfort dripped off him
    like crude turpentine, pungent and pale yellow. Because my mother
would not approve, we stole there in secret, my father and I,
    early one Saturday to the cramped space of his projection booth
before the first matinee. Light bounced off the tin walls
    from the projector's lamp fierce as my will to win. His Sanderson
fixed on the tripod, me pert on a stool, dark hair in waves tumbling
    past my shoulders. He stroked his hair, fiddled with the camera,
told me to reposition, to look away from the lens. Instead I looked
    at him. Treat me like an object, I said, not unkindly. He shook
his head, then nodded. So much had come to bear on this moment,
    on this contraption of metal, wood and glass, the whole town
willing me gone for good. I make folks restless with a sideways
    glance, a lift of chin, so this language of expression is something
I believe in, and needing more than luck, I ignored my father
    and stared into the perfect eye, casting thoughts like spells
into the little magic box: *Olive's shoulder, Theda's smolder,*
    Gish's sweetness, Griffith's weakness, little incantations until
the room began to topple, the smell of silver so strong
    my mouth burned with the taste of it and my heart burned
with the taste of it as I offered everything I knew to this eye
    that would know what to make of me. *Mabel's smile, Norma's style,*
Mae's pout, Pickford's clout. My image seared through the lens,
    through the film, forged a hole to another place, forged a tunnel
until I could find my way clear and my dear father, and the world
    I left behind would fit in the palm of my hand.

My Mother Tells Me I Was Conceived in Fire before I Was Condemned by It

I was admiring the trimmings in O. L. Keenes,
the lace, the ostrich feathers in pale colors. Was it
the steam whistle I noticed first, grey clouds
rolling up from the ground? I don't remember.
The city was imperiled. From the doorway, I saw
flames in the northwest moving at a gallop.
It was terrifying. Bay Street filled with people
heading east, I joined them, passing families laden
with mirrors, dishes, children leading dogs on strings,
carrying bird cages, so many horses and drays loaded
down with trunks, me holding only a pale pink feather,
worrying how I'd pay for it now.

At Monroe Street,
unable to help myself, I turned around to face the blazing
pursuer. Angels of oblivion pummeled toward me
on billowing, black smoke, like an engraving by Doré—
this nightmare rendered so precisely.
Isn't it magnificent? I said to a man nearby. His eyes
considered me. They were oddly green, like verdigris
and heavy-lidded.

Sparks landed like confetti, but long I was willing
to stay there and watch this parade of danger so close
he brushed it from my hair and I brushed it from his sleeve,
before he clutched my hand, pulled me with the others
past Hemming Plaza, into the Windsor Hotel crowded
with the displaced, belongings stacked everywhere,
then down a corridor into a room.

Even when the door clicked shut, I thought of him
as protector while wondering who would save me now.

Ostrich feather gripped in my hand, I did all he told me to do.
Why I never let it go. Why I never fought at all, but laid there
long after he left until smoke filled the room clearing my head
and I fled with hundreds of other bodies, empty-handed
out of that hotel, each of us racing in the direction that felt right.

Toward the river I ran. Across it was this house, untouched
and I wondered if William was imagining me dead.
At the dock I turned around one last time, and this is what I know of Hell:

The Windsor had become a furnace, radiating heat far and wide,
the flame of its burning ascending towards Heaven, groaning
with a thunderous voice in its agony. The steamer pulled
away and a dead moccasin floated by. Another then another
and another and another. What to make of it, I didn't know.
As though it was a sign that evil had been vanquished.
But it hadn't been. It burned inside and half the sky was on fire
and what trees remained in the distance looked like skeletons
and everyone on the boat was cast in the strangest yellow light,
like none I'd ever seen, altering features until any one
of the passengers could have been him.

Still riding the billows of smoke like clouds,
the angel of oblivion appeared to me and in my own bed
that night. Awake or dreaming, it was a true vision all the same.
I was with child and this one would live. She smirked at me

and the clock read 11:00 exactly and your father's face
(*your father's face?*) was bathed in that same yellow glow
and it was more than I could bear. I turned from him
and pressed my hand to where it hurt and was horrified grateful.
Looking at you now, I'm horrified grateful.

At church, in a park, on the trolley,
when I see men that resemble my memory of him—
a grey serge suit, drowsy-lidded eyes, a cleft chin,
to this day I want to ask: *Were you that stranger?*
Were you that stranger? Please, tell me your name.

THE SNAKE MAN CONSOLING

With ashes make a poultice
and put it on a wound. Spread them
at your threshold and pests won't linger
at your door. But don't strew ashes carelessly
in the yard, although the chickens will bathe
in them, they will kill the camellias and a host
of other good things. Set some aside to leaven bread.

The venom from a diamondback relieves
arthritis and gout. With it I make medicine
that waylays the cancer and induces dreams
that lead you back to things you thought
were lost forever. But if that snake bites you
directly, your leg will grow round as a tree trunk
and dark, your eyes will quiver and your heart will beat
itself against your ribcage trying to get out.

What can kill you in one form might save you in another,
but it ain't nothing that can deliver you from yourself entirely.
Some people get redeemed in the river, others just drown there.

At the Station

I kissed my father and held
his two hands in mine.
They were cracked like fallow land,
so dry. His gray eyes, clouds.

I hugged a lamppost goodbye
or perhaps that was my mother.
There is no give to her.

Ladies from the church brought
sandwiches and prayer
made stale by circumstance.

Dulcie stood behind them,
waiting her turn, hand
deep in her pocket. Closer
she came and blew ashes in my face,
then wiped her hand on my hair.
It wasn't anything I could refuse her.

I conjured Henry's face.
His blue eye a pool, the other
one a well where I tossed handfuls
of recompense and made a wish.

My eyes stung, I licked my bitter lip.
The taste of rue and pine,
I heard the lamppost say.

ON THE TRAIN TO HOLLYWOODLAND

For five days I didn't exist anymore,
suspended like a wire between a life
that had ended and one not yet begun.
We passed through towns, across
trestles into parlous terrain I couldn't
make sense of. Unrecognizable,
the faces around me.
An aloneness so peculiar—
to not know tree or sign, a stranger
to every person. Instead of free
I felt as expendable as chewing gum.
I'd grasp the *Photoplay* contract
for something akin to solace,
tried to rest. It declared me
a winner, but promised little else.
Bouncing and lurching toward panic
as we headed west, the train tracks
disintegrating behind me, I fell
in and out of fitful sleep until the dust
that was the tracks drifted
onto my dreams where they grew
larger than my leaving and seeped
a shade of red I'd felt, but never seen.
Open your eyes, a signpost read.
*The land is awash with the blood
of dreamers. Open your eyes,*
the Snake Man said.
My body was a string plucked
awake to a sea of flowers
that beckoned then parted before me—

a mass of poppies crowding
the rails all the way to yonder!
Like nothing I could have imagined.
Like Heaven opening its arms.

The Devil's Passkey

The shoe poised on the tip
of my toe was a lure. Even
directors important as
von Stroheim want
to be hunted. *You there*
(eyeing my ankle,
my nearly exposed foot),
you can dance? I nodded.
And like that I became foreground,
in his second film. *The Devil's Passkey*
boasted stars who spurned my display
as if they'd only known fullness
their whole lives. But I knew better.
Opportunities are rare as rain
out here, even for beauties
knocking on closed doors
day after day, shoes and skin
coated with dust. Some days
that dust was the only thing
in our bellies, those of us
who didn't come floating in
on a raft of our father's money
or favors due. So I let my
feet be bathed on film,
my toenails painted—I danced
barefoot on a table then dangled
my legs off the arms of some
actor who flourished me
around like a prize. Later, von Stroheim
would go over the reels and reels

of footage (so to speak)
and afterwards take me with him
to the Ingress where the beautiful
and newly rich gazed and grazed.
Beneath the table I'd rub my stockinged
foot along his leg and when I stopped
he'd press his leg against mine
and we'd pass the evening rubbing
and pressing while introductions were made
to men who might be inclined to help me.
They handed me their cards like keys. *I can open
many doors, they'd say. So many doors . . .
I have many doors to be opened,*
I'd whisper, *I may let you enter all of them.*

FRAY

Fits were thrown
and often hammers
while sets were built
and directors demanded
focus from a face
that wouldn't wince
from hissing lights
that burned our eyes
and skin, requiring
poultices of potatoes
and gauze, but later,
because now a baby is yanked
from my arms,
crying for his bed,
it's night though lights
make it day and exacting
voices yell for me
to pull my hair then
clasp my breast then
wring my hands and tear
at the clothes
of the welfare dame—
your baby in her grasp,
drop to your knees—
look down, down, but still
plead, *now Lyla move*
your head up slow, no,
that's too slow, shadows
make hags of girls, you know
that—now the tears, Lyla,

give me tears, stare into the camera
as though it were your dying ma—
suffer, suffer, ignore that laughter
from the other set,
just Roscoe taking one
more pratfall for the day,
now get up and hotfoot it
after them, tripping over your baby's
rattle—we couldn't have planned
that better, Lyla, now make it hurt
enough for the girls in the back row,
yes, real blood on your lip,
that's the way, crumble
as that door slams behind them,
that's the way, now strain
for the rattle just out of reach,
strain harder, Lyla, harder,
hold it hold it hold it AND—collapse.
Take a few, but don't freshen up.
We're building a ledge
for the scene where you jump off.

On Being Given a Monkey
Fur Coat from a Suitor

I asked L at what point did savages think
a species once tamed, could always be tamed?

I've read we're all descendants of a wild stock.
I've had feral thoughts, a tendency to regress, an urge

to swing from tree to tree. With hesitance I
come down. Domestic races have a monstrous nature.

This monkey fur coat has sleeves that drip tresses
more lustrous than my own hair. Too beautiful

to let be, I suppose. Or too valuable. Darwin said it was
absurd to talk of one animal being higher than another.

How easy it would have been to charm him, show him
how to use his long beard like a feather. Degeneration

happens with a breath, a button. I'm a testament.
A hierarchy of beauty exists. This coat is a vestment!

A struggle for dominance inevitably followed.

THE SOUBRETTE TAKES CENTER STAGE

—*Photoplay, May, 1921*

In her first major role Lyla Dore will further
prove to her fans why she's a star on the rise.
Those eyes! That hair! Those gams! It didn't
take von Stroheim long to see that Lyla in the
background is just too distracting. It's hard to
focus on the star with Lyla's radiance stealing
the scene. Now she has to prove it to the nay-
sayers who declare she is only one more
exceptional face in a town brimming over with
them. This is make or break for Lyla. Von
Stroheim can be a dictator and doesn't suffer
foolish girls gladly. It's even been said he is
a Svengali. But Lyla is spirited, as proven by
her nights on the town with a host of handsome
and powerful men. I'm told that a certain married
leading man has not stopped sending her flowers
since sharing a dance with her at The Ranchero
two weeks ago . . . When asked about her upcoming
role in von Stroheim's latest project, she admits
to being nervous. She knows the public is always
looking for a new face and she hopes hers has
the staying power of a Lillian or Gloria or Pola.
As far as working with a director as demanding
as von Stroheim, Lyla replied, "I don't mind being
told what to do by a man. As long as it's the right
man, I rather enjoy it. After all, he sees what the
camera sees. He is the first, best audience and if he
is pleased, I know I will be too." At that she crosses
her enviable ankles and blows a kiss toward our
appreciative photographer, who I'm certain would
be willing to do whatever she tells him!

Angel's Tit

—1/2 oz. maraschino liqueur, 3/4 oz. fresh cream,
maraschino cherry garnish

Not thriving, I had to think of myself
as a commodity, contrive ways to get
noticed, get close enough to discern
what makes a particular man hum.

I devised a special calling card.
A dance around the floor
of the Century Club one evening
may earn me an afternoon
appointment with a certain director
the next day. I'd show up with a box

from the bakery and when admitted
to his chamber, I'd ask him directly
and without guile if he was in the mood
for dessert. And well, if there was no
interest, there was still cake.

Most often, there was both.
A bit of icing rubbed here
and there . . .
It was effective and—
who doesn't like cake, after all?

> *(A bit*
> *of cream*
>
> *on the tip*

                    a pit both sweet
                              and hard your tongue

                         a butterfly that flits
          from bud to bud taking

                         small sips your lips

            again your lips
                              bring nectar down

                    to our fingertips)

Gifts followed as well as parts
that would have only gone
to someone less
creative. The stories became
legend, and at C's behest
a libation was concocted
in my honor. Would-be
starlets loved to be seen
ordering and sipping
from a drink they had
no idea was named
especially for me.

WHEN HENRY CAME TO TOWN

I'd heard there was a new cameraman
in town with an eye patch and looks

to spare, a real baby, talent to boot.
Father mentioned in a letter last month

that Henry headed west with the other studio
folks who'd all closed up shop back home.

I waited outside of the Triangle Studio's gates
for two hours until I caught sight of him.

Unreadable was his face, he looked neither
surprised nor unsurprised to see me or even

startled by the ground that shook beneath us.
It was curious, the closer he came, the farther

away he felt and the chasm too great for me
to cross alone. My hand offered to him,

I caught myself, pulled back, tried
to say his name, but it just echoed against

the chambered walls of my hollowed-out heart.
Henry Henry Henry Henry Henry

Flux

For weeks it was nearly
impossible to sleep.

The earth swept
wildly beneath

my bed. I felt
the moon's pull

in my marrow,
the ebb and flow

of regret. With my hands
cupped like delicate

seashells over my ears
I could hear my blood

rush, then sigh—
the burden

of my heart. Little
fist clenching,

replenishing its sweetness,
transfiguring its sorrow.

Go On, Please. This Is Very Interesting

Old antics couldn't be helped. Those minutes
were a determined hand. Cupped,
ready to be filled. A bowl

on a table, a perfect peach inside.
That's what reason is. I ate it,
but I'm still hungry for all the good

things trouble has to offer. It needs
sweetness. Trouble does. Like bugs
on fruit, their bodies so small

they're colorless, don't even
have a name. But enough
of them could devour you.

My real name makes me sound like a maid.
And not a good one. A fetcher,
a plodder. Feeling my way along

the unglamorous dark wall of someone
else's room. Delivering useful things,
like towels. Relentless drain

on my own life. Hot days I lie
in my dry bathtub and read.
Bare skin on porcelain stays cool

and who wants to turn pages
when wet? I imagine someone
watches me, leaning back on a pillow,

holding the script my body
at a certain angle. Hips rounded,
I make a shallow bowl of my belly.

I am my own best audience.
I said bowl before, didn't I?
Lying there, lying here.

It feels like that sometimes.
Like I'm never alone with myself.
Like all my moments play out

just ahead of me.
Does that make you think
we're getting somewhere?

I wish I'd known beforehand
how far it would go.
M once called me treacherous.

Like a cliff, he said. *Your edge appeared*
sound, but you gave way beneath me.
And him. And him. And him. And him.

My skin that peach gives
just as easily. I suppose
my time is up.

But there are days when
everything feels like mine.
Even what is yours.

This Is How It Ends

As they're dying, I want my lovers to think of me,
my hair draped silk across their chests,

my calculated breath creating small summits
of skin I conquered many times before

in Catalina, the Garden of Allah, balconies,
desks and office couches. Reverie will tempt

their tongues to slip through lips like small snakes.
I'm the charmer urging their mouths into a parting kiss.

Careworn wives think they need a drink, offer ice chips
and rest sad hands on their arms, heavy as overripe pears.

But they turn away, move toward the fragrant shade
of memory's hair. Sweet like orange blossoms.

Behind my ear it's white as orange blossoms.
I'm the secret you will keep from this world

spills from my mouth in soft petals. My face dissolves
into so many petals, they cannot blink them away.

The Last Veil

It's the dream sequence
that's regarded most,
Raoul was a director
who understood how fully
an audience will lose
themselves in a moment,
knew how to exploit it
and with this film
he made me a star.

No favors had passed
between us, without pretense
he *chose* me for the role
and it felt like the world
had finally shifted back
into a place that didn't upend me.

Lew Cody played the married man,
dreaming he was a king. More
handsome in person than any
photograph ever captured, still, he had
the breath of a rhinoceros that day.

The costume was only veils,
seven of them, bejeweled
and sheer, reaching the floor.
The king looked bored when I
began the dance, more interested
in the pretty girls that stood
next to him holding his cup

and fan, but as I twirled
and swayed around him, my
hips expressing their own
usefulness, his eyes widened,
taking in my ankles, my legs
as I removed the first
then second veils.

I moved closer to him and off
came another until my knees
were exposed, and then another
and another and restless
he became in his seat, eyes fixed
on the sixth one. I peeled it off slowly,
dropping it around his shoulders and
revealing my thighs like exotic fruit,
the audience's breathing
as labored as Lew's, I'm told.

Left with one veil draped
around me like a near-nothing
toga, I danced over and around
him, moving away, then closer,
away, then closer, until he reached
out to grab me, but seized only
the end of the veil. I leaned in

to kiss him, but when his lips
neared mine, I pulled back,
twirling madly, his hand

still holding onto the cloth
so that the more I spun the more
naked I became, whirling into
the shadows and out of the frame,
no one could see anything,
but the idea of it was enough.
And as I neared the edge
of the screen, audiences,
from Tupelo to Tacoma,
jerked their heads to the right
as if I'd continue
spinning into their aisles,
as if that last veil
was the only thing
that kept us apart.

WHEN HENRY BROKE THE SILENCE

Even in shadow I knew it was him.
Silhouette so sensible, just outside
of the streetlight, leaning
against his car. Stepping out
of my Duesenberg, I felt silly,
leopard-skinned upholstery,
a champagne dress held fast
by diamond straps. All affectation.
Moorish mansion on the hill
behind us, garish backdrop,
a fan club's idea of a movie star's life.

He was immune to it, I suspected,
having lived and worked among the airs
and graces for several years now.
Nonetheless.

It was yet a small town then
and though our paths never crossed
they sometimes paralleled.
I wanted to ask why he was there,
but this moment felt thin as crystal.

It's Dulcie, he said.
I looked down,
because what could I say?

*She writes to me regularly,
hates that I've made my home
in this "cemetery of virtue."*

Morning and night, she prays
for me, but says God
won't answer those prayers
until she reveals her truth.

The fire was Dulcie's fault, Willie.
She left a candle burning
in her room too near
a curtain, went downstairs.
Everyone else in bed.
There was a shift of wind
and by the time she knew
what was happening,
the upstairs was consumed.
Nothing she could do,
but walk out the front door,
unable to close it, though no one
was coming out behind her.
All the same, Willie,
she still lays the blame with you.
Says you were the shifting wind.
You were the errant flame.

I didn't ask what he thought.
There was small solace in this
confession, save the presence
of Henry on my street.
Beyond him was only darkness
and we trembled there,
both of us breakable.

I have no one here. Nothing
that connects me to the person I
was when I came into this world,
except you. It was his voice,
but he was speaking the words
in my own heart.
Such melodrama, too great
even for me. But I succumbed
to it, flung myself against him
like a penitent, holding fast
until he granted me an embrace.
The little patch of light we shared
beneath the streetlamp felt like an island
we were stranded on. I closed my eyes
against that light and prayed no one
would try to save us.

For Henry

As children we passed many lovely days
together, so easy it was between us,
that I mistook it as ordinary. How could I
have known? You were a gift
I received too early—I wanted a toy,
but was given a golden ring.

I've known what it is to be adored, to wear
professions of love and desire like a coat,
but still feel the chill of loneliness
in the warm breath of others.

With you it's as though a balloon
has been blown up inside of me and pushed
to the outer edges of myself, I'm filled
with a happiness I could burst from.

I once asked you to explain what all of this amounted to.
You answered with certainty, *It's a love story.*

Hold my hand and that happiness,
weightless and potent will lift us
up and over bygones, beyond fates.
Let me live with you there.
In love's enduring,
golden story that knows
no beginning and will not end.

The Snake Man and the Pearl

And he spoke plainly, calling me from the fullness
of myself in sleep, saying, *You have sheen, Willie,*
like the inside of an oyster shell, you still glow.

The Snake Man's hand shaped a breeze that brushed
the hair from my eyes, still I wouldn't open them.
His voice was a siren's voice, leading me to a craggy past.

At the border I thought he'd left me, by the poppies
and the train tracks. Years had passed without him
until it all seemed like a dreaming. *But one night*

you were only shell, he said. *Underneath that house,*
emptied. Beneath my eyelids I felt a burning,
as if from sand and I knew he put it there

so I would blink and see what he wanted me to see.
On the ceiling a perfect circle of shadow moved inside
the moon's reflection. *You thought everything had been taken,*

but something was left there, a bit of grit. The circle shifted
and a profile emerged, long hair, bangs, a turned up mite of a nose.
And from that grit came pearls, Willie. A life for you and a life

that goes on despite you. "She is seven!" burst from me
and the room, like a sinking boat, filled up with a sorrow
I heaved on, choked on, until I gave in and let it suffuse me

and the drowning grew peaceful. A question I'd never asked
had been answered. Words I hadn't conceived of welled up
in my throat, spilling out, "She is seven. Her hair is long and I know

her eyes are green. That nose is my mother's nose. I've seen her,
so many times, in the shadows of little girls skipping on the lot
or playing in front of a store. She exists, has always existed."

In this way I grieved what I knew, but didn't know
at the same time, holding both of those things
in my outstretched hands as I watched her on the ceiling,

kneeling, her hands rising and falling in small gestures
like she was playing a game of jacks or Pick-Up Sticks.
My dark pearl, my luster of shadow.

The Snake Man stroked my arm until she faded
and I drifted away from the rocky shore. *Mother of Pearl*,
he whispered over and over. *Mother of Pearl. Mother. Of Pearl.*

He slid my eyes firmly shut as if they were latches on a door.

This Is How It Really Began

In a grove of orange trees, a girl is hiding.
The rain is coming toward her.
She can see it just across the road.
She waits for it to come, but it stops right in front of her.
She reaches her hands into it.
She leans her face into it.
She stands sideways so that half of her gets wet and half of her does not.
She laughs and her voice is thunder.

In this way, the girl first begins to expect an extraordinary life.

This Is How It Really Ends

Not in a puddle of my own blood, not in a dismal
studio apartment, not behind a perfume counter
in a second-rate department store.

When I could have utterly ravaged my soul
I made some good choices, wise investments.
Not to say there weren't too many times
in the early years, when I would get lonesome loaded,
seek out the warmth of anything that felt like desire.

Those days I had a custom of stealing a token
to remember a tryst—a cufflink, a fountain pen,
a handkerchief, a golf tee. What it was I wanted
to later conjure, I'm not certain.
Perhaps it was a way of keeping track,
of making those hours mean something.
I kept the treasures in an ivory box (a box I took)
and would look at them from time to time
until the weight of them grew heavier
than my ardor. I buried it then on the backlot
at Universal and a week later was given
my first real role in *Sins of the Father*.
Everything changed after that.

I presume it will be said of this story,
there is too much guilt and not enough gilt.
Of the latter much has already been said.
Another catalogue of movies and accolades,
of escapades and jewelry is not needed.
Those will endure without me.

But I digress.

This is about endings which really are only the start
of something new. Talking movies aren't a fad,
despite what friends want to believe. Their ears so full
of sand. Am I ready to stop making movies? No. And no.

But times have changed, films move on.
I would have to reinvent myself and I've made such a mark!
To continue feels impossible knowing what I become
would always be compared to what I was before.
Younger girls, with a different style, flair. It's grown daunting.

So, this is how it will end, with my head on the chest
of the man I love in a comfortable bed, in a palatial
home, the sound of the ocean beyond our window.
It feels like the edge of the world.

When I can't sleep, I think
of my sweet, dead father, of Mrs. Moore
and the twins. I think of my own child who never knew
my touch and my mother who's softened in age,
though warily, and Dulcie. When I can't sleep, I think
of a tortoiseshell toothpick, a tiepin, a fork
from the Coconut Grove. I imagine a young woman
uncovering that box of fetishes, each token held
to the light, examined. She stares at the golden tiepin,
its ruby center an eye that beckons her,
the charm that will change her days.

Some nights I call out in a whisper, *Snake Man, Snake Man.*
I watch the shadows move along the walls, wait for him to speak.

Magic Lantern *Reprise*

In a room with a white wall, my mother waits
for her dying day, silk cord tied to her wrist
and to my father's magic lantern on a rollaway cart.
She gazes at slides, Delilah shearing Samson's hair,
miniature poodles jumping through hoops, her at a picnic,
me riding a bike. She pulls the cart away from the wall until
it looks as though I'll ride right over her.
Then she pushes it closer and the tunnel of light
grows small and I all but disappear.

Strange, the things that make a heart feel glad.

Star Dust

Combusting into dust, we were
brittle kindling it seems, flash
of light, pile of ash, disintegrating
into nothingness so easily.

We were supposed to be
immortal there, on our own
little planet of nitrate and silver.

Instead we were the experiment
sent to prove life could exist,
could subsist on light and adulation.

Imagine! A whole industry built on beings
worshipped from afar! Lonely,
but lucrative, it ended not with a boom,

but with static, low and persistent
that seemed to come from some
place even farther away.

When we first heard sound stumble past
our own lips, it startled us all.
We'd only wanted to be seen, not heard.

Eventually we were neither. Only specks
of light suspended in the ether, suspended
in a silence that will never be seen again.

THE SNAKE MAN AND THE
GHOSTS OF BEAUTIFUL WOMEN

They go right on as they did in life—
never opening a door or paying
for a darn thing. They show up
at all the best parties, the best
restaurants and still make fools of men—
pour salt in their bourbon, untie
their shoes, unzip their zippers,
and pull their chairs away.

Of course, they had to adjust
their methods. Once they could
merely fix their gaze, steady
as a pilot light, to get a man's
notice, then turn the flame down
or up to make him behave or
misbehave, depending on their mood.

What fun it had been! The gifts
they'd received! But memory is just
a reminder of how they've been reduced
to slapstick for attention. Dispirited,
they leave the noisy parties
and restaurants to find refuge
in tall trees at the edge
of town where roosting
like egrets, curling in
on themselves, they debate
whether their lives served
any purpose beyond
the ornamental.

By and by, each offers up
some specific moment
as proof and yes,
they finally decide,
yes, there was purpose,
there was meaning.
Even so,
anyone walking past
would be bowled over
by the enormous moon-
flowers aglow in the tree
and think to themselves,
how beautiful they look,
and how out of reach.

Notes

When Kalem Studios Came to Town
Details from this poem were suggested by titles of silent films made by Kalem Studios in Jacksonville as well as a serialized article, "Blazing the Trail." *Woman's Home Companion* (Nov. 1928), written by Gene Gauntier, a scenario/script writer and actress with Kalem Studios.

Phantasmagoria
Images from this poem are derived from the work of the artist Lindsay Packer (www.lindsaypacker.com).

A Visit from the Snake Man
Although the Snake Man is a fictional character, he was suggested by a photo of real person, Cy Foreman, who was a resident of Jacksonville, Florida and was known as the Snake Man for the elixirs and medicines he made from snake venom.

At Kalem's Headquarters, the Roseland Hotel
The idea of this poem was derived from the serialized Gene Gauntier article, "Blazing the Trail." *Woman's Home Companion* (Nov. 1928), and G.W. "Billy" Bitzer's writings about camera and lighting experimentation in the early days of silent film.

THE FILMING OF THE CLARION

Information found in *The First Hollywood* by Shawn Bean (University Press of Florida 2008) and *Almost Hollywood: The Forgotten Story of Jacksonville, Florida* by Blair Miller (Hamilton Books 2013) helped with the writing of this poem.

WHEN THEDA BARA CAME TO TOWN

Eve Golden's *Vamp: The Rise and Fall of Theda Bara* (Vestal Press 1996) provided inspiration and information for this poem.

MY MOTHER TELLS ME I WAS CONCEIVED IN FIRE BEFORE I WAS CONDEMNED BY IT

Some details and descriptions of the Great Fire are taken from Benjamin Harrison's account in *Acres of Ashes* (East Florida Printing Company 1901).

ON THE TRAIN TO HOLLYWOODLAND

The final lines of the poem are paraphrased from a quote by the silent film actress, Leatrice Joy, in the documentary *Hollywood: A Celebration of the American Silent Film, Tape 2, In the Be-ginning* (Dir. Kevin Brownlow and David Gill, Thames Television, 1980).

THIS IS HOW IT REALLY ENDS

A moment in this poem was suggested by the documentary, *Mary Pickford: The Muse of the Movies* (Dir. Nicholas Eliopoulos, Earthlight/White Castle Productions, 2008).

BIOGRAPHICAL NOTE

Teri Youmans Grimm is a fourth generation Floridian. She received her BFA in poetry at the University of Nebraska at Omaha and her MFA at Vermont College. Her poetry collection *Dirt Eaters* was chosen for the University of Central Florida's contemporary poetry series and was published by the University Press of Florida. Her writing has appeared in *Prairie Schooner, Green Mountains Review, Indiana Review, South Dakota Review, Connecticut Review, Sugar House Review, EAT* and *Homegrown in Florida: An Anthology of Florida Childhoods*, among other journals and anthologies and she is a contributor for the podcast Swamp Radio. She is the recipient of a Nebraska Arts Fellowship and has been awarded residencies at Virginia Center for the Creative Arts and the Hambidge Center. She teaches in the University of Nebraska at Omaha's low-res MFA program. Teri lives in Jacksonville, Florida, with her husband and two children where she sings in a cover band and hunts alligators. Visit her website at teriyoumansgrimm.com.

CPSIA information can be obtained at www.ICGtesting.com
Printed in the USA
BVOW00s0540201016

465544BV00001B/7/P

9 781597 093224